Christmas Recipes From the Past

Over the centuries, immigrants have brought Christmas traditions from around the world to the United States. Many of the recipes in this book come from other countries. As our country grew, these new traditions spread quickly. Folks used to visit each other more often, sit a spell, and enjoy homemade desserts in the parlor. Food is a celebration to observe each day!

Snow Cream

Ingredients:

snow (or finely crushed ice)
sugar
red and green sprinkles
heavy cream
vanilla

Directions:

Scoop up some clean snow from outside. Place in chilled bowl. Add cream, sugar, and vanilla. Mix and freeze for 5 minutes. Blend in red and green sprinkles. Serve frosty!

Old-fashioned Pull Taffy

A classic Victorian Christmas included several parlor games, decorations, special foods, and of course, the time-honored tradition of pulling taffy. Children liked to see how long they could stretch the taffy until it broke. This old-fashioned recipe promises loads of sticky fun!

Victorian Pull Taffy

Ingredients:

2 1/2 cups sugar
1/4 cup vinegar
1 T. butter or margarine
red and green food coloring
1/2 cup water
1/8 tsp. salt
1 tsp. peppermint extract

Directions:

Combine first 5 ingredients in a small Dutch oven; cook, without stirring, over medium heat just until mixture reaches soft crack stage (270ºF). Remove from heat. Stir in peppermint. Add red food coloring to one half and green to the other.

Pour candy onto a well-buttered 15 x 10 x 1-inch jellyroll pan or slab of marble. Let cool to touch; pull candy until light in color and difficult to pull. (Butter hands if candy is sticky.) Divide candy in half, and pull into a rope, 1 inch in diameter. Cut taffy into 1-inch pieces. Wrap each piece individually in waxed paper. Yield: about 40 (1-inch) pieces.

Stained Glass Cookies

Old European churches were often built with beautiful stained glass windows. Artisans created the windows to resemble religious images like Christ, the apostles, or other biblical events. Many churches host elaborate Christmas celebrations each year.

Stained Glass Cookies

Ingredients:

Pre-made sugar cookie dough (keep refrigerated until use)
1 bag sour-ball candies (assorted colors) or
3 packs of Life Savers (assorted colors)

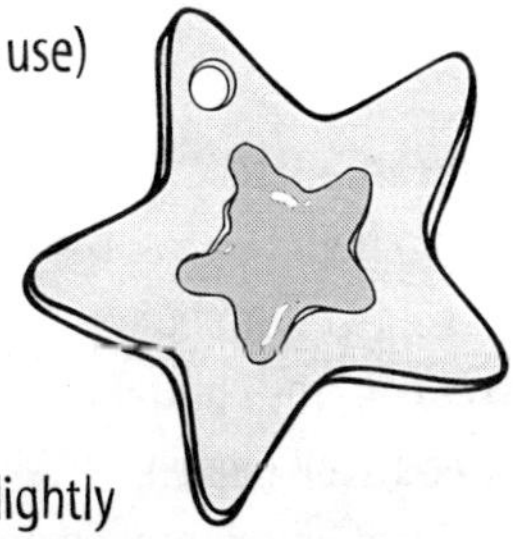

Directions:

Preheat oven to 350ºF. Line two baking sheets with aluminum foil. Roll out pre-made cookie dough on a lightly floured surface. Use cookie cutters to make shapes from the dough. Then cut a tiny shape (like a circle, heart, or lines) in the center of each cookie. Don't cut to close to the edge, or cookies will break. Collect scraps of dough, roll it again, and cut more shapes until all the dough is used. Make sure dough stays cold. Separate the candies by color and fill a plastic bag with each group. Wrap one bag in a dish towel and crush the candies with a hammer. Repeat process with each bag. Candies should be 1/4" pieces or smaller. Fill the cookies with the pieces. Carefully place cookies on the baking sheets. Bake for 10-12 minutes. Cool for 10 minutes until candy hardens. Then peel cookies from foil. Store in an airtight container.

Sugar Plum Pudding

From Jack Horner to Jack Frost, everyone loves to eat plum pudding at Christmastime! Plum pudding is one of the oldest and most traditional Christmas desserts. In the 17th century, English families called it "hackin" pudding because it had so many ingredients! Plum pudding was sprinkled with brandy and served flaming in its dish!

Sugar Plum Pudding

Ingredients:

- 1 cup flour
- 1 1/2 tsp. nutmeg
- 1/2 cup fresh butter
- 1 egg, well beaten
- 3/4 tsp. cinnamon
- 3/4 tsp. soda
- 1/4 cup sugar
- 1/2 cup buttermilk
- 1/2 cup plums, cooked and chopped

Directions:

Preheat oven to 350ºF. Mix flour, spices, and soda.
Add butter to dry ingredients. Add the sugar and mix well. Add eggs and buttermilk to the plums in a separate bowl. Add this mixture to the dry ingredients. Mix well. Pour into a buttered pan and bake until done.
Bring 1/2 stick butter, 1/4 cup buttermilk, and 1/2 cup sugar to full rolling boil. Remove from the heat and add 1/4 tsp. pure vanilla extract. Pour over the pudding.

Swedish Cookies

In Sweden, Christmas is celebrated from December 13 (Lucia Day) to January 13 because of an ancient royal decree. On Lucia Day, the eldest daughter, dressed in a white gown with a crown of candles, welcomes the Christmas season by awakening her parents with the song "Santa Lucia." She brings them coffee, buns, and cookies.

Swedish Snaps

Ingredients:

1 cup butter, softened
1 1/2 T. molasses
1/2 tsp. ground cardamom
1 tsp. baking powder
2 eggs whites, lightly beaten
3/4 cup sugar
2 tsp. ground cinnamon
1 T. water
2 1/2 cups all-purpose flour

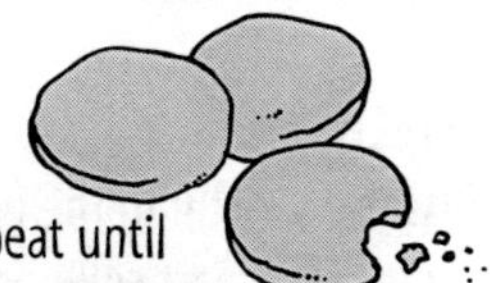

Directions:

Beat butter (medium speed) until creamy. Add sugar, beat until smooth. Add molasses, cinnamon, cardamom, beat until blended. Combine water and baking powder in a small bowl. Stir until baking powder dissolves. Add to butter mixture. Add flour gradually, beat until blended. Cover; chill for 8 hours. Roll dough on lightly floured surface to 1/4" thickness. Cut out Christmas shapes with cookie cutters. Place dough shapes on greased baking sheets, 2" apart. Brush shapes evenly with egg whites. Sprinkle with white sugar. Bake at 375°F for 8 minutes. Cool on baking sheets.

Moravian Christmas

At Christmas, Moravian churches host "love feasts" where people gather to sing and share coffee and buns. In the Middle Ages, Morovian priests displayed hand-carved nativity figures to tell the Christmas story. Moravians came to America for religious freedom in the 1700s and brought this Christmas "putz" tradition.

Moravian Love Feast Buns

Ingredients:

- 1 qt. warm milk
- 1 1/2 cups sugar
- 2 tsp. salt
- all-purpose flour
- 3 yeast packets
- 3/4 lb. butter, softened
- 3 tsp. cinnamon

Directions:

Dissolve yeast into the warm milk. Add 1 T. of sugar. Mix yeast solution with the rest of the ingredients. Add enough flour necessary to make a soft dough. Knead dough on a floured surface and place in a bowl. Let the dough rise until it doubles in size (about an hour). Form dough into small buns and place on greased baking pans. Let the dough rise again.

Preheat oven to 375°F. Mix up a bit of glaze by beating sugar, egg yolk, and milk together; lightly brush over buns. Bake until brown, about 30 minutes.

Christmas Fruit Cake

During the Middle Ages, people loved to eat lots of delicious dishes at Christmas. Mince pie, which included various chopped meats like partridge and rabbit, was a favorite. Later, the dish became a pudding when sugar, raisins, and and candied fruits were added. Christmas fruit cakes evolved when dates and nuts were included.

Christmas Fruit Cake

Ingredients:

- 5 large eggs
- 1 cup white sugar
- 1/2 tsp. baking powder
- 1 lb. glazed pineapple
- 1/2 oz. vanilla extract
- 1/2 lb. butter
- 1 3/4 cups all-purpose flour
- 3/4 lb. glazed cherries
- 4 cups chopped pecans
- 1/2 oz. lemon extract

Directions:

Cream butter and sugar until fluffy. Add well-beaten eggs and blend well. Chop nuts and fruit and mix with part of the flour. Sift remaining flour and baking powder. Then fold this into the egg mixture. Add flavorings and mix well. Then add fruit and nuts. Mix well by hand. Put mixture in a greased tube pan. Place in a cold oven. Bake for three hours at 275ºF. Then let it stand until it's cool.

Gingerbread House

Gingerbread houses are a popular Christmas tradition. Families like to make them together. You could make a log cabin, dog house, Santa's village, a church, or even the White House! Be creative!

Gingerbread House

Ingredients:

1 egg
3/4 cup + 1/8 cup packed brown sugar
1 tsp. allspice
1/2 cup butter
3 cups all-purpose flour
assorted candies for decorating
1/4 cup honey
1 tsp. cinnamon
1 tsp. ground ginger
1/2 tsp. cardamom
1 tsp. baking soda
1 1/2 cups powdered sugar

Directions:

Heat oven to 350°F. Stir butter, powdered sugar, and honey over low heat until melted. Mix flour, spices, and baking soda into a bowl. Add melted mixture and egg. Mix everything and knead into a ball. Chill dough for 30 min. Roll dough flat until 1/4 inch thick. Cut cardboard patterns for the walls and roof of house. Press patterns on dough and cut around edges. Set pieces on baking sheet; bake 20 min. until firm. Let pieces cool. Mix 1 1/2 cups icing sugar, 3 T. meringue powder, 1/2 tsp. cream of tartar, 1/2 cup warm water in chilled bowl until smooth. Use icing immediately (it dries quickly) as cement to build your house. Decorate with licorice, candy pieces, candy canes, pretzels, cinnamon dots, marshmallows, lollipops, coconut, and cookies!

Norwegian Cookies

Norwegian immigrants brought a special, deep-fried Christmas cookie called fattigman (futty-mun) to the Midwest when they came to America. The word fattigman means "poor man's cookies." When you make this dessert, you are reminded to remember people who are less fortunate than you. Help someone have a joyful holiday season!

Norwegian Cookies

Ingredients:

6 egg yolks
1/2 cup cream
1 tsp. nutmeg
2-3 cups all-purpose flour
powdered sugar
1/3 cup sugar
1 tsp. brandy extract
1/4 tsp. salt

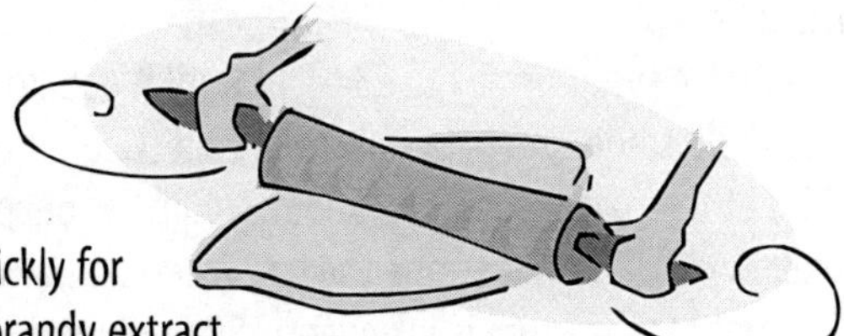

Directions:

Beat egg yolks and sugar quickly for five minutes. Stir in cream, brandy extract, and nutmeg. Mix in enough flour to make a stiff dough. Roll dough very thin and cut 2" square pieces. Cut a slit in the middle and pull one of the square's points through the slit. Ask an adult to deep-fry the cookies until they turn golden. Cool cookies and sprinkle generously with powdered sugar.

Maple Cream Candy

Maple sugaring is a big part of American history! In fact, Northeastern United States and Southeastern Canada are the only places in the world where maple syrup is produced! Each spring, when the temperature is above 32°F in the daytime and below 32°F in the evening, sap travels up and down maple trees, which are then tapped. Sap is then made into maple sugar and syrup!

Maple Cream Candy

Ingredients:

1 quart Grade A maple syrup

Directions:

Boil maple syrup briskly to 234ºF, or until it gets to a "soft-ball" stage. Keep crystals from collecting on the sides of the pan. Pour syrup about 3/4 inches deep into a shallow dish. Do not scrape the pan when pouring syrup. Cool until the mixture is lukewarm. Stir with a spoon until light and creamy. Pour the mixture into a greased dish. Let it set, then cut it into small squares. You can also make maple cream candy shapes by using well-greased Christmas cookie cutters. You'll make 2 pounds of maple cream candy!

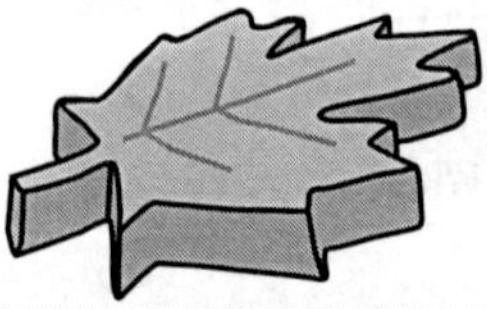

Here We Come A Wassailing

In the old days, families would gather around the fireplace to drink hot cider or chilled eggnog at Christmas!

Holiday Eggnog

Ingredients:
3 cups whole milk, 1 cup heavy cream, 1/2 cup sugar, 4 large eggs, 2 tsp. vanilla extract, freshly grated nutmeg

Directions:
Whisk milk, cream, sugar, and eggs together in medium saucepan. Cook over low heat, whisking constantly until mixture thickens slightly (5 minutes). Do not let it boil. Remove from heat and stir in vanilla extract. Refrigerate egg nog. If it thickens, add a little milk. Serve chilled and topped with nutmeg!

Hot Apple Cider

Ingredients:
1 quart cranberry juice, 1 quart apple juice, 2 oranges, zested, 14 whole cloves, 1 1/2 cups dried cranberries, 1 tsp. vanilla extract, 1 1/3 cups honey, 2 cinnamon sticks

Directions:
Pour cranberry and apple juice into saucepan. Cook over medium heat. Add orange zest, cloves, cranberries, vanilla extract, honey, and cinnamon sticks. Heat until hot and steamy (about 20 minutes) & stir occasionally. Serve in your favorite Christmas mug!

Southern Christmas

These traditional Christmas recipes originate in the Deep South where peanuts and pecans reign supreme!

Nutcracker Pecans

Ingredients:
1 1/2 quarts large pecans, 2 1/4 cups sugar, 2/3 cup water, grated orange rind

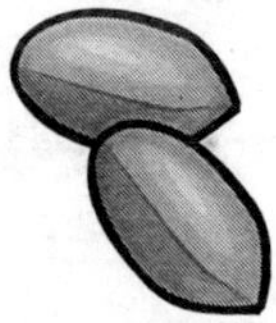

Directions:
Mix sugar and water. Boil until syrup spins a thread. Continue cooking until mixture reaches soft ball stage. Remove from heat and add grated rind. Stir until it gets foamy. Sir in pecans, coat well. Pour into lightly greased dish. Separate pecans with fork while syrup is warm. Let pecans harden and cool.

Peanut Brittle

Ingredients:
1 cup sugar, 1/2 cup white Karo syrup, 1/4 cup hot water, 1 tsp. butter, 2 cups raw peanuts, 1 tsp. soda, 1 tsp. pure vanilla

Directions:
Bring syrup, sugar, and water to a boil. Add butter and peanuts. Boil and stir constantly until the peanuts start to pop and the syrup starts to brown. Remove from the heat and add vanilla and soda. Work fast! Pour on a greased marble slab, smooth out, let cool. Break into large chunks.